HEADING

RUGBY FOR AMBITIOUS YOUNG PLAYERS

FOR THE TOP

Heading for the Top

HEADING

RUGBY FOR AMBITIOUS YOUNG PLAYERS

FOR THE TOP

Kerry Wedd

Foreword by Jack Rowell,
Coaching advice and contributions from
Brian Ashton and Richard Greenwood

With acknowledgements for special assistance to Alan Barter, Michael Raw,
Dr. Norman Healey and Jonathan Wood. Contributions from Dean Richards,
Phil De Glanville, Rory Underwood, Mike Catt, Rob Andrew, Kyran Bracken,
Tony Underwood, Neil Back, Jonathan Sleightholme, Jonathan Callard,
Lawrence Dallaglio, Graham Rowntree, Grahame Dawe,
Martin Johnson, Ben Clarke and Tim Rodber.

International photographs by Russell Cheyne (courtesy of the *Daily Telegraph*)

Quiller Press
London

Heading for the Top *is for ambitious young Rugby players – 12 to 16 group.*

The book looks at the skills and the learning necessary to achieve success. It offers encouragement and experienced advice from some of the very best players and coaches in the land. Every chapter is headed by one of the top England players – competitors who have had to strive to achieve such standards.

Heading for the Top *shows that with perseverance, every ambitious young player can improve his performance. Above all, it underlines the enjoyment of being part of a worthwhile team game.*

The Coaching Edition *of* **Heading for the Top** *– is available by the same author. Specifically written to raise standards in the 12-16 Group game, the author includes coaching contributions from Brian Ashton and Richard Greenwood – both top line players and International coaches.*

First Published 1997 by Quiller Press Ltd, 46 Lillie Road, London, SW6 1TN

Copyright 1997 © Kerry Wedd

ISBN 1 899163 32 8 – paperback
ISBN 1 899163 35 2 – cased coaching edition

Designed by Jo Lee
Printed by Colorcraft Ltd, Hong Kong

CONTENTS

ACKNOWLEDGEMENTS

My sincere thanks to all who have helped to bring these pages together. I acknowledge especially the expertise of **Richard Greenwood** and **Brian Ashton** – both top line players and International coaches in their own right; also of **Michael Raw** and **Alan Barter** – former colleagues on the coaching team at Sedbergh – who have re-written parts of the text and made various suggestions. My thanks to **Jack Rowell**, to members of the **England Squad** and to photographer **Russell Cheyne** for their contributions to this project. I welcome this opportunity to express my debt to numerous coaches, colleagues, former pupils and parents whose support and friendship over many years has been so important; especially to **Jonathan Wood** and to **Sarah** for their constant encouragement.

Kerry Wedd, 1997.

Photographs
Senior players courtesy of the *Bath Chronicle*, the *Daily Telegraph*, the *Leicester Mercury* and Rhino Rugby. School boy shots taken by Anthony Moseley and Charles Price at Mount House School, Tavistock.

Special thanks to: Tim Buttimore, Derek de Glanville at Rhino Rugby, Charles Price, Headmaster of Mount House School, together with coaches John Symons and Geoff Whaley and their young players.

Proceeds from the sale of this book will be donated to **The Wheels Fund.** Providing modern facilities for disabled children, the project is undertaken on behalf of **SPARKS** and **The Lord Mayor Treloar School**, Nr Alton, Hampshire. (See back cover for further information.)

FOREWORD

By Jack Rowell

I am pleased to add a few words to this excellent publication for ambitious young rugby players seeking to improve their performance.

Our sport continues to grow rapidly. The arrival of professional rugby has brought many of the world's top players to our shores. The success of the latest British Lions Tour in South Africa will ensure further promotion of the game. For UK enthusiasts there is the prospect of World Cup 1999, with the final to be played at Cardiff. We have much to look forward to...

Rugby players today are taking part in a demanding, fast moving game – one in which the traditional roles and playing styles of forwards and backs have evolved and moved on. Our leading senior players now possess more uniform and interchangeable playing skills – underpinned by increased thresholds of physical and mental preparation. They are top class athletes in their own right.

With such an abundance of interest and enthusiasm evident, this young players' guide not only brings sharp focus to the game but also provides an update on key skills, knowledge and motivation. The material which follows has been drawn from a number of current international players and top schools' rugby coaches. I encourage all ambitious young players to study the contents carefully.

It is also well worth noting that, whilst striving for excellence, the book emphasises ingredients of fun, fair play and friendship which are so much a part of this game.

JACK ROWELL, England Manager

Paul Grayson v. Scotland 1997.

THE GAME OF RUGBY

66 *To fully appreciate Rugby Union, you need to experience the lofty moments of success as well as the morale bending lows of defeat; you have to feel the hard graft of training sessions and to share some of the team struggles which unite players. With the onset of the professional game, players have had to re-double their efforts to improve personal fitness and the game has become faster and more demanding. Often it takes a deal of grit and*

determination and unless you are willing to work hard at the game, you'll be wasting your time. If you are fortunate though, you will find yourself part of that special spirit which comes to a group or team striving together towards a common goal.

Rugby has given me many very good years. In the early days, as a working man with a young family, the game was never my whole life; I always kept other interests – and I think that this may have helped me to enjoy playing more than most. Rugby has been a source of much pleasure and many good friendships and I would certainly recommend it to any young person who is looking for a worthwhile sporting challenge. 99

DEAN RICHARDS
Leicester, England and the British Lions

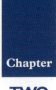

YOUR PERSONAL APPROACH

66 *Before going any further, it is important to establish your personal approach to the game – your attitude, your temperament, your commitment. You need to determine just what you really want from rugby and just how much you are willing to sacrifice in order to achieve this goal. Each player must make his own decisions.*

Phil De Glanville at Twickenham

For many young players the answer may not yet be clear. You will have various options and prefer to keep interested in a number of sports and other activities. You wish to enjoy your rugby but have not yet decided, finally, if this is the sport you wish to follow more seriously…

There is no urgent rush and many very good players do not take up the game until long after the age of 15.

However, if you are ready to make your mark in the game, I recommend careful study of the sections which follow… 99

PHIL DE GLANVILLE.
Bath and England

HEADING FOR THE TOP *contains advice and support from players who have experienced the international game; not so long ago we were all of us ambitious junior players like yourself. It is our hope that these chapters will encourage you to raise your sights – to realise that you can do a great deal to improve your game if you have the right approach…*

i – SKILL AND FITNESS LEVELS

We must all start here. Certainly, you won't make much of this game without putting in a lot of work on your personal fitness and skills – and the sooner you can set yourself some clear targets the better… *(Chapter 3 on Fitness… gives a good outline of what you need…)*

ii – DETERMINATION

No-one gets to the top, in any sport nowadays, without a deal of dedication. It has to matter to you and you must be willing to stick at it until the results begin to come. Essentially, you've got to enjoy the challenge of self improvement…

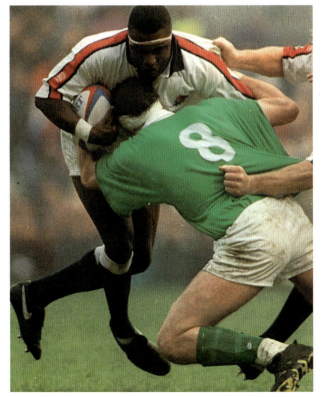

Steve Ojomoh v. Ireland. Strength and determination

Just how determined are you?

Are you a once a week player or will you put in the extra hours of practice to improve, whatever the weather? Are you prepared to work at it or do you expect immediate success? Are you easily discouraged or have you got the grit to succeed?

How determined are you?

iii – TEACHABILITY

Some young players learn quickly – some don't; some listen carefully – some don't… What about you?

iv – LOVE OF THE GAME

Some thrive on the competitive contest; on the raw challenge of pitting skills against others – your strength or endurance or cunning against theirs. Some thrive as part of a Team.

3

Jonathan Sleightholme v. Wales 1997. England's powerful winger on his way to score again.

v – KNOWLEDGE AND UNDERSTANDING

It is a sound policy, sometimes, to put yourself into the position of **Captain** or **pack leader**; this way you begin to see more clearly the strengths and weaknesses which matter most; you realise that enthusiasm without understanding can be a real problem.

First and foremost, the captain's job must be to draw the best out of his players. At Under 16 level, he must accept that the **Coach** will play a vital role and that the successful partnership between player and coach is very important. Between them, they will agree the **Action Plan** – the plan which will determine how best to use the available players.

Check List

Try giving yourself a score of 0–10 against each of the following headings… A score of less than 5 in any section is too low for an ambitious young player. Over 5 for each section would suggest that you are ready to read on…

Skill	/10
Fitness	/10
Determination	/10
Teachability	/10
Love of the contest	/10
Support for the coach	/10
Positive attitude	/10
Sportsmanship	/10
Understanding & Knowledge	/10

SUMMARY...

So, back to the three key factors:

ATTITUDE – TEMPERAMENT – COMMITMENT

What do you really want from rugby and just how much are you willing to sacrifice in order to achieve this goal?

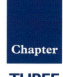

ARE YOU FIT TO PLAY RUGBY?

**Including: A) Do you Know? – Ten questions on fitness,
B) Understanding Your Own Individual Programme, C) Test Yourself**

66 *Ambitious young players must understand that the modern game demands new levels of fitness. This chapter is written for young players who are seriously considering more demanding training programmes.*

Top-line sports people realise the need for a programme which balances hard physical exercise with the benefits of developing mental strength, and a sensible life style. Any player who can learn to take responsibility for part of his own training will be taking an important step towards success…

A pause here to ensure the right approach may save you hours of wasted effort. 99

New Zealand All Blacks on Tackle Bags.

**KERRY WEDD and
DR. NORMAN HEALEY**

A FITNESS GUIDELINES FOR YOUNG PLAYERS

Question 1: *Why do I need fitness training? I am a naturally fit person; I play quite a lot of games and I wonder if I really need any more fitness training…?*

Answer: Sensible question. You need to work at the right programme – but, certainly, all the other games will assist your fitness.

Your reasons for special fitness training are:
i) to prevent injury by increasing your ability to recover and by increasing flexibility.
ii) to build up endurance so that you can stay at your best, without flagging, for the whole game.
iii) to increase sharpness (speed, acceleration or decision making…)

Question 2: *Do I need to bother with special pre-season or out of season training?*

Answer: Yes. Most young rugby enthusiasts will enjoy a number of different games which will keep them reasonably fit. But Rugby fitness is not the same as, say, Swimming fitness or Athletics fitness. If you want to make the most of your Rugby potential then you will need a sensible pre-season/off-season programme which prepares you for the rather special demands of the game. Once the match season begins, you will be busy improving skills and team work; it is therefore essential that much of the hard, endurance training has been completed before your season starts. Senior players call this "money in the bank".

Question 3: *What sort of pre-season training do I need?*

Answer: Endurance work; flexibility exercises; speed training. (See **Individual Training Programmes** at the end of this chapter…)

Question 4: *I need to get bigger, stronger and faster. How do I do this?*

Answer: By following the guidelines here… Avoid the "get strong quick" adverts and learn more about the facts of how your body works. The essential point to understand is that your system needs to develop gradually – and the training programme must allow this…

Now read on…

Austin Healey (Leicester, England and the Lions) – one of the quickest scrum-halves in the game.

Question 5: *What about weight training?*

Answer: Heavy lifting work, weight training or repetitive "slog" training sessions are not recommended for the Under 16 Group. The basic reason is that until your bones have hardened or developed (usually at about 17 years of age) you can cause injury or upset to the growing process. Certainly, you would do well to seek expert advice before you include serious strength training in your private programme. In other words, concentrate on **Skills**, and on the recommended exercises for now. Strength training will be vital, but not yet.

Question 6: *Does this mean that I shouldn't drive myself really hard?*

Answer: Not at all! It simply means that you must allow recovery periods for your growing system. By all means, train hard and stretch yourself to the limit but (a.) allow recovery time and (b.) avoid slogging away for hours at strength exercises. Your policy should be to train hard for short, sharp sessions of an hour or so. Concentrate on skill and speed improvement at this age and save the serious strength training until you have stopped growing… As a general guideline: "If it's not fun, then there's probably a better way of doing it!" Take a day off after a really tough session and come back to it when you are fresh. In common with other top-line athletes, get your regular sleep.

Question 7: *What about diet?*

Answer: Good nutrition is important because it helps you to recover between training sessions. You certainly do not need to become too fussy about what you eat but you may find the following suggestions are helpful…

i) **Eat plenty of carbohydrates** – the fuel foods. (Bread; rice; pasta; potatoes + fruit and vegetables. Breakfast cereals are good for you at any time…)

ii) There is good sense in **cutting down on fatty foods** and too much chocolate – but the key word must be "sensible" not "faddy".

iii) Variety in your diet allows you to enjoy your food and to get the most out of it.

iv) Try to take some water or a soft drink before and immediately after strenuous exercise.

Question 8: *Eating before a match?*

Answer: Not a big problem. **Eat a little of whatever you like**.

Ideally, give yourself a gap of an hour or two before you play – but it's really a matter of finding out what suits you. You obviously don't want a huge meal just before a game! Once you have eaten, try to relax for a while, to allow digestion.

The old idea of "a steak before a match" ran into difficulties when it was discovered that it took 12 to 18 hours to digest! You would be better off with a couple of bananas, a sandwich and a muesli bar! Some players prefer toast and honey…

Question 9: *Mental preparation?*

Answer: I cannot over-emphasise the need for sensible mental preparation. You have decided that you want to play well – so prepare for it. Teach yourself to concentrate before and during the match. Think about your role as part of the team. Get your mind alert to what may be required and, above all, be positive – not negative. Prepare yourself to achieve, not to fail. Give yourself a quiet period before the match…

Mental preparation takes the stress out of the moment, allowing you to concentrate, ready for what's ahead. You want to be relaxed but ready for action. There's no need for frowning and growling, over-aggressive threats or head-banging…

Question 10: *Should I have my own individual programme?*

Answer: Yes. Every individual will be different. What works for others may not be right for you. Get some assistance when planning your programme – but the following guidelines may help…

What do you really want from rugby…?

B UNDERSTANDING YOUR OWN FITNESS PROGRAMME

Many young players will be forced to train away from the facilities of Club or School. You won't go far wrong if you include three types of training in your general pattern...

FLEXIBILITY • SPEED • ENDURANCE

Where possible, train with at least one partner

I FLEXIBILITY

Always start here...

You are recommended to include flexibility exercises or stretching exercises every day – even on non-training days. It makes good sense to begin every session with gentle stretching in order to bring the muscles into use gradually. The "stretch" should never be savage – "mild discomfort" being the absolute limit. It must be a gradual stretch – not a jerk. Hold each position for a few seconds...

After a hard match or work out it is an aid to relaxation if you can spend a few minutes working through your range of flexibility exercises.

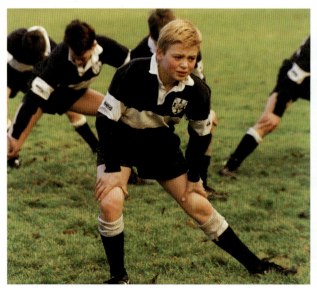

Flexibility – always start here.

Three of England's quickest. Nick Beal with Tony Underwood and Jeremy Guscott in close support.

2 SPEED TRAINING

There is no substitute for pace and all players should work to improve speed. As the competitive season gets closer, you need to "speed train" several days a week. You won't become a top-line sprinter over-night but you'll be surprised what regular, quality training can do... If possible, obtain the help of a qualified Athletics Sprint Coach...

Many rugby groups use "**Winders**".

On the Rugby field – **Walk** (try line to 22 line); **Trot** (22 to half-way); **Stride** (half-way to try line). Walk back to start again.

As the fitness increases, cut out some of the walking and lengthen the sprints. In early training, ensure that the "walk" sections are long enough to allow you to maintain quality in the sprints. Without quality, it's not worth doing...

Each length of the field is know as a "Winder". 20 hard Winders gives a good test of anyone's fitness...

You will read about top athletes using "bounding" or "rebound" training and this will probably form a part of your Club sessions when it can be fully supervised.

8

3 ENDURANCE

Your ability to keep going for long periods without losing your skill level. This endurance must be built up over a long period of time – months not weeks… It fits well into the off season period.

Steady running of 1 to 3 miles – several times a week. Run in pleasant surroundings if you can – on the beach or in the hills – but do it! You are building up basic endurance which will be vital later in the season…

Targets should not be based on age alone; height and weight need to be taken into account

What sort of scores should I get?

Take the tests and record your own set of results. Your first fitness Target is to improve your own performance.

But, be aware

It is quite usual to improve steadily when training sessions begin, but **be prepared to reach the first "rest phase" or "no progress" stage.** This is a period when many uninformed young athletes lose heart and believe they will never improve any further. Stick at it for several weeks and gradually you will work your way into the next "growth phase". Be aware that growing, like learning, tends to improve in steps – followed by rest periods.

Training must be purposeful; it can also be fun

C   TEST YOURSELF

Your individual fitness programme.
Start by testing yourself on the five listed exercises...

You need to be fully warmed up before tackling these exercises

1. The Shuttle Run – (Agility and Speed.)

- Take two points, 5 or 10 metres apart. (The closer the points, the more of an **Agility Test** it becomes...)
- See how many times you can "Shuttle" back and forth between the two points in, say, 30 seconds.
- Record your score. Rest for one minute and then repeat.
- See if you can maintain "good form" for 5 runs.
- Ideally, your partner will take turns with you. Time each other; compete with each other.
- But try to keep the rest periods to the same, precise time …
- As you get fitter, you can increase the Shuttle Sprint time or distance.

We want "electric pace over 10 to 15 metres"

2. Power Jump – (Leg power.)

There are two good Leg power checks:

i) **The Sergeant Jump** – an upward standing jump. Measure the distance between the highest point you can touch from a standing position, to the highest point you can reach with a standing jump.

ii) **The Mat Jump** – a standing mat-jump for distance.

- Lie on your back on the mat. (Heels right on the edge of the mat – not beyond.)
- Chalk mark the mat as far from your feet as you can reach with both hands.
- Standing jump from just off the mat. Measure the distance from chalk mark to heel.

You should be able to leap your own height and beyond...

3. Pull Ups or Press Ups – (Shoulder strength.)

It's very simple to cheat!
Decide for yourself what, precisely, you mean by a Press up or a Pull up.

- **Press ups** require a full dip to the ground. **Pull ups** require the chin to touch the pull up bar with no assistance from a body swing or a kicking action.

Both exercises will give you a shoulder strength score to improve upon.

4. Trunk Curls – (Abdominal or Stomach strength.)

There are numerous ways of measuring abdominal strength. A simple test is all you need.

- Lie on the mat. Using stomach muscles (not arm movement) sit up far enough to touch knee-caps.
- Lie back again – until head touches mat. Repeat sit-ups as many times as possible in 30 seconds.

5. Endurance Run – (Your ability to keep going...)

- Decide your own distance run – somewhere between one and three miles. It can be round a field or out on the cliffs...

Time yourself over the run and then over a period of weeks, enjoy seeing that time improve.

KEEP YOUR OWN FITNESS RECORD

Record your individual results and try to improve in one month's time

Name

Position Chosen

	Date 1	Date 2	Date 3
Age			
Height			
Weight			
1. Shuttle Run (Agility and Speed) (2 points, 10 m apart)			
2. Power Jump (leg power) (Sergeant or Mat Jump)			
3. Pull Ups or Press Ups (Time limit of 30 seconds)			
4. Trunk Curls (Abdominals) (How many in 30 seconds)			
5. Endurance Run (3 or 4 laps of the field)			

INDIVIDUAL SKILLS FOR ALL PLAYERS

Including: A) Confident Tackling, B) The Skill of Passing, C) Taking the High Ball, D) The Defensive Fall, E) Play Touch Rugby League, F) Kicking Skills, G) Know the Penalty Laws

MULTI-SKILLED PLAYERS

" *Today's game requires all members of the Team to be multi-skilled. Backs must be ready to help their forwards with rucking and mauling; forwards must be quick enough and skilful enough to join the threequarter line whenever needed. All players should be comfortable about their role in attack or defence…*

This section looks at skills which every up and coming young player should try to improve… and don't forget the Penalty Laws. "

RORY UNDERWOOD
Leicester, England and the British Lions

THE INDIVIDUAL CHALLENGE

" *The individual challenge of one against one is perhaps the most compelling reason for playing this game. This chapter lists a number of skills which can help all young players – but, remember, there's no substitute for superior fitness and sheer pace. If you are serious about becoming a top-line player – get yourself fit first…* "

MIKE CATT
Bath, England and the 1997 Lions

CONFIDENT TACKLING   A

In this chapter we have placed Tackling first on the list. Learn to tackle properly and you will feel confident to go on and build up all the other skills.

There are different situations when a slightly different tackle is required; where details are bound to alter slightly according to circumstances – but if you can concentrate on these essentials they will improve your game...

i) Tackling is about **Timing** and **Body Position** every bit as much as it is about **Bravery** and **Aggression**.

The basics include:
Head up – eyes on the target.
Head behind; drive hard into the tackle; grip tight and hang on firmly until the man is fully down. Prevent the pass if possible; if the ball goes loose – we want it...
You must get to your feet before you can play the ball.

The tackle from behind.

ii) For the more advanced tackler –
Be in contact with the ground as you drive into the tackle. You want to be moving forwards and upwards into contact; use your studs to generate push, drive and lift. Aim beyond the man...
(By getting close to your opponent before the drive, you reduce the risk of being side-stepped or beaten by a change of pace. By driving upwards into the tackle, you are lifting your opponent and can then take control over how and where you want him to land.)

iii) **Practise** first with a tackle bag or a willing partner. Use matting and walk-through pace until you have really mastered the skill. Feel the difference between tackling from a distance (just out of range) and tackling from close. Feel the power when the tackle comes from leg strength...

iv) Tackles to master –
Tackle from the side – tackle from behind – smother tackle – head on tackle (shown below).

Confident tackling, timing and body position.

B   THE SKILL OF PASSING

1. Power comes from the wrists – with the thrust being exerted by the flick of the two small fingers as the ball is released…

2. The ball should be held and received away from the body – to ease quicker passing…

3. Keep the ball always at finger tips…

4. Look at the receiver and pass a metre in front to allow him to take at speed and with arms away from his body…

Will Carling shows perfect timing v. Scotland.

C   TAKING THE HIGH BALL

Every player is required to deal with the **High Ball** from time to time. It may come from the opposing kick-off or it may be that you are covering in defence. Usually, the **Full Back** or **Winger** will come from behind and call for the ball – in which case your job will be to give him immediate support, from behind.

However if it is your High Ball:

i) Get underneath it. Call "My ball!" loudly enough to convince everyone that you mean it. Try to turn side on to give yourself a really strong, wide base. Where it is possible, position yourself to react with a kick or a move but usually it will be a matter of staying on your feet until your support players arrive. Turn also to prevent a nasty knock as your opponent follows up. Catch with the whole body – not just with your arms. Cradle the ball and make it yours…

ii) The more advanced player will also wish to practise the safe catch high off the ground. This is more difficult.

Right: Taking the high ball. One advantage of taking the catch off the ground is that you should not be tackled while in the air…!

Only come off the ground if you know that otherwise an opponent will reach the ball ahead of you. You want the same strong, side on catching position – only this time you want it several feet off the ground.

Again, concentrate on catching with the whole body – not just reaching up hopefully with the arms. The key lies in making the ball yours and then coming down into a crouch.

As you land, you have to be rock solid and on your feet, ready for an opposing tackle or for your own supporting players…

iii) Practise on your own to begin with. Then get a partner to toss the ball and follow up, gradually building the pressure.

THE MARK

A "mark" is really a defensive call, usually made by the Full Back or Wing man as the ball is caught. it must be called inside the defenders' 22 and is used when the alternative is to be tackled in possession of the ball. Both feet must be firmly on the ground as the mark is called. (A leap to catch the ball as in the photograph on the previous page is of no use if a mark is intended.) The referee needs to satisfy himself that the catcher is in full control – otherwise he will allow play to continue. Once called, the catcher should never assume that his "mark" has been accepted until he hears the whistle. Many a Full Back has been flattened after an unsuccessful mark…

To mark the ball, you must have your feet firmly on the ground.

THE DEFENSIVE FALL   D

The ball is loose on the ground behind your players, probably not far from your own try line. You are the first defender to arrive. You have time only to hurl yourself onto the ball, just ahead of the attackers who wish to hack the ball onwards…

Much depends on the firmness of the pitch. If it is wet, it often becomes a "defensive slide" rather than a "fall". The basics remain the same – and apply to all players.

i) Eyes on the ball; back towards opponents; cradle the ball – pull it in to your body and then try to get to your feet. The law is clear: you must get to your feet or release the ball **immediately**. You cannot afford to give away a simple penalty.

As your skill improves, try to gather the ball and get up in one single movement.

ii) As you get to your feet you are almost certain to have to cope with an aggressive opponent who will try to rip the ball off you or turn you towards his own support players. Again, as with the **High Ball**, you want a strong, wide base which allows you to hold on until your own support arrives.

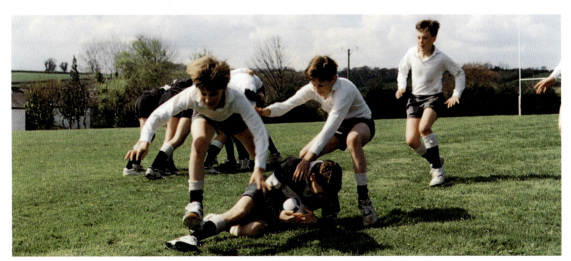

E TOUCH RUGBY LEAGUE OR SEVENS

I want all players to become skilful handlers; confident about giving and taking a pass and expecting to score tries… For this reason, I include **Touch Rugby League** in almost every practice session, whenever there is a gap in the 15-a-side match programme.

If you stick to the rules, it is a game which can be played with or without an adult referee. It can be played on grass, on tarmac or in a Sports Hall.

Try the following basic rules:
- Non tackling. (Unless you have an adult referee.)
- Best with no more than 6 a-side.
- Touch on shorts or below. Two hands touch.
- Touched player must stop, roll the ball back between his legs.
- Player who picks up must pass immediately.
- Defending team must retreat 5 paces (or be at least 5 paces back from the break down.
- Use the 22 or one half only.
- Agree the rules before you start! Appoint your chief official!

Good tactics to encourage:
- Two quick passes away from the break-down.
- Insist on space between teams at break-downs.
- If the defending team does not retreat 5 paces – the game will not work!
- Always go forwards; make your support runners run off you.
- Keep the ball alive…

F KICKING SKILLS

Paul Grayson v. Scotland. One of the best kickers in the game.

All young players should try to become competent **Touch Kickers** but I also like to include **Place Kicking** as part of the **Skills For All** approach.

TOUCH LINE KICKING

There are certain essentials to follow:
- Place the ball on your foot – don't drop it.
- Eyes on the spot you aim to kick.
- Head down – and keep it down – right into the kick.
- Follow through. Kick right through the ball.
- With care and skill you can add the **Screw** or spin to the ball – but the same basics hold.
- Practise both left and right foot touch kicking.

Head down…

Eyes on the ball – head down – good follow through.

PLACE KICKING

Make yourself into a top-line **Place Kicker** *and you will be worth a place on most teams. It takes dedication and many hours of practice but there are a number of helpful guidelines to follow:*

Take care how you place the ball. Get right down, behind and low, when you line the ball up precisely as you want it. You don't need more than 4 or 5 paces for a run-up.

"Round the corner" or "straight through" kickers require:
- Eyes on the spot you aim to kick.
- Head down – and keep it down – right into the kick.
- Perfect balance.
- Follow through; right through the ball.
- Check the position of your stud marks after the kick…

Spend time experimenting with the best way of placing the ball. Try the different foot positions – toe-kicking through the ball or round the ball as shown. Study the experts…

KICKING PRACTICE

Use a line for practice.
Kick for accuracy to a partner. Start close and move back as you become successful.
For serious practice/competition: use the Try Line. Try to bounce the ball back off a single post target. First to score 5 hits is the winner.

Excellent balance…

17

G   DO YOU KNOW THE PENALTY LAWS?

Why give the game away?
Few mistakes are more infuriating to a coach or a captain than those of a player who hasn't bothered to learn the Laws.

As an ambitious player, you need to ensure that you know what a referee must penalise…

a) In the Scrummage, you should be penalised for:
i) not binding properly; you must have a genuine grip.
ii) deliberately collapsing the scrum.
iii) using a hand to help the ball out of the scrum.
iv) breaking away from the scrum before the ball is out.

b) In the Lineout for:
i) Holding down an opponent.
ii) Barging the opposition out of the line.
*ie. There should be no contact until the ball has been touched by the jumper… (At the time of printing, the Law does **not** permit **Lifting** at Under 15 level…)*

c) On the Ground:
i) Lying in a way intended to stop the opposition from winning the ball.
ii) Handling the ball again after you have been tackled. The Law says that you must first get to your feet…

ie. If you're on the ground, you're out of the game. You must get to your feet before you play…

d) At the Tackle:
i) High tackle. Neck or dangerous tackles should be penalised.
ii) Late tackle/Early tackle. The player must have the ball in his hands…
iii) On the High Ball. You may not tackle the man whilst he is still in the air.
iv) Obstruction. Deliberately blocking a tackler's way.

e) Off-side:

Most penalties are given against off-side players.

In simple terms, **a player is offside in general play** if he is in front of the ball when it was last played by one of his own team. He need not be penalised unless he plays the ball or approaches within 10 metres of an opponent waiting to play the ball.

A player is offside at a scrum if he joins from his opponents' side. Any non-scrummager must remain behind the back foot of the scrum. The player putting the ball into the scrum is offside if he places one foot in front of the ball while it is in the scrum. Back-row forwards must stay bound until the ball leaves the scrum.

Offside at ruck or maul? You may not join the ruck or maul from your opponents' side; if you are caught out of position, you must immediately retire.

Any player not joining the ruck or maul must remain behind the back foot… (NB. at the kick-off…)

Offside at the lineout? Players not involved in the lineout must remain behind the imaginary 10 metre line until the lineout is over. (The thrower and the scrum half are regarded as being "involved"…)

The lineout ends when one of **four** things happens:
i) the ball touches the ground,
ii) the ball is passed back out of the lineout,
iii) the ball is caught/held, a maul is formed, and the whole "scrummage" has moved away from its original position…
iv) the ball is thrown beyond the 15 metre line.

Penalties are so influential in the modern game that I strongly recommend players to list situations or incidents which resulted in a penalty either for or against. Learn to beat the penalty count and you will be a long way down the path towards successful rugby…

Note that **Free Kicks** (**not** penalties…) are awarded for:

i) Closing the gap in the lineout too soon;
ii) Standing up in the scrummage (usually the Front Row who are in trouble…)
iii) "Not straight…" – in lineout or scrummage.
iv) Accidentally off-side.

Is this a ruck or a maul? see page 52, quiz 2 (3).

19

IMPROVING THE HALF BACKS

THE DECISION MAKERS...

66 *Half Backs provide a vital link for successful rugby; they bring together the threequarters and the forwards. Many of the most important team decisions come from this pair – to spin the ball wide; to break from close in; to take the ball back into a strong pack or to kick for position... Half Backs must be willing to take responsibility and to enjoy the challenge of directing the game...* 99

ROB ANDREW
England and the British Lions.
Now Coach to Newcastle Gosforth.

THE HALF BACK PARTNERSHIP

66 *The Half Back partnership is crucial. It is a very demanding position, both in attack and in defence. At International level, things tend to happen pretty quickly and it is a huge advantage to be familiar with your partner's game – to know how the other man is going to react under pressure situations.*

I particularly enjoy Scrum-half play because it keeps me in the centre of the action. It is my job to provide quality ball for my Outside Half, but I also share many duties with the Forwards. At any level, the more you can practise, and play together under match conditions, the sharper you should become.

Any ambitious Half-back will benefit from a careful study of the skills and practices listed in this chapter. 99

KYRAN BRACKEN
Saracens, England and 1997 Lions

i – THE OUTSIDE HALF

You're fortunate if you have the ability to play in this key position; it requires a great deal of skill and dedication to reach the higher levels. Where possible, we will look for the running game, with the Outside Half as the man who sets his runners free. The secret lies in timing; in choosing the right option.

It is commonly believed that **"great outside halves are born – not made…"** but here are seven guidelines which will help any ambitious young player.

  Take time to understand them.

i) The Outside Half moves as the ball leaves the Scrum Half's fingers – not before.

ii) Try not to run across the field. (You will remove space from your centres and also make an easy target for the opposing open-side flanker…)

iii) You want the ball into your fingers; in front of you without over-stretching for it.

iv) If you aim to make a break yourself – you want the ball flat; if you aim to move it wide, you still want the ball flat but you may pass the ball to a player who is deeper… (see diagram below Flat or Deep pass.)

v) Your running line should be such that you stop the first defender from moving sideways across the field. (ie. It is your job to "take out"/occupy the first defender…)

vi) For defensive purposes, you are often best placed directly behind your Scrum Half.

vii) Communication is vital. If you aim to kick, you will be almost stationary and your Scrum Half needs to know… Use agreed hand signals – not shouted instructions.

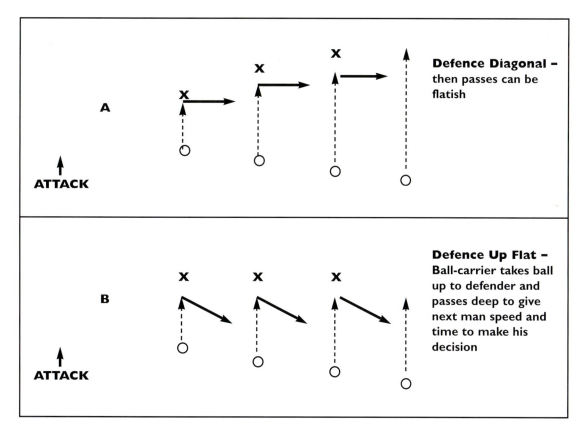

A

ATTACK

Defence Diagonal – then passes can be flatish

B

ATTACK

Defence Up Flat – Ball-carrier takes ball up to defender and passes deep to give next man speed and time to make his decision

So much depends upon your opposition positioning. If the opposing defence is up flat on you, then you may have to pass a bit steeper; if the defence is well back then you can stay flat… Think about it…

ii – THE SCRUM HALF

Make no mistake, yours is, perhaps, the most influential single position on the field. Not only will you need to possess more than your share of energy, skill and understanding of the game, you must also be a decision maker and a communicator. A silent Scrum Half is seldom doing his job; he must often be "the eyes of his forwards"…

(Scrum halves need to practise as much with the **Hooker** and with the **Number 8** as they do with the Outside Half – see chapter 6C on Scrummaging…)

Concentrate first on perfecting the really quick, standing **Spin Pass** *off either hand; then work on the* **Dive Pass**, *to be used under pressure… A scrum half with the pace off the mark to make an occasional break is a huge asset. (Note: "occasional".)*

a) The Spin Pass
- Start with a stationary ball and a stationary target.
- Aim to hit finger tips – at waist height – every time.
- Rear foot immediately behind the ball.
- Get low – over the ball, knees bent, eyes on the ball, weight on the back foot… Avoid backlift…
- As the controlling hand moves in behind the ball, your weight will shift into a good stride towards your target. (The other hand is merely a stabiliser…)
- The controlling hand stays in contact with the ball as far down the pass as is possible.
- Spin is imparted by pushing the control hand right through the line of the ball; it is not necessary to twist or strain.
- Be prepared to practise with and without the space/time for the back lift or pick up.

Andy Gomarsall v. Scotland

Spin Pass series.

b) The Dive Pass

The Dive puts a Scrum Half out of the game for an instant and should therefore be used only under pressure. (ie. moving away from fast closing opponents).

- Start with a stationary ball and target.
- Begin several paces from the ball.
- First foot goes immediately behind the ball.
- Eyes on the ball for the pick up.
- Keep hands/ball back as far as possible before the actual delivery.
- Short pace before dive/drive away from opponents.
- Drive forwards and up. You must give yourself height to have time for a really accurate pass.
- The skilled passer will be able to develop a **Diving Spin Pass**

A good example of the Dive Pass.

iii – COMBINING THE HALF BACKS

The Outside Half takes responsibility for his positioning and for the speed at which he wishes to move on to the ball. He must be in total control of whatever option he decides to take next.

It is the Scrum Half who must deliver the ball in the correct position, immediately it is available. Just as a Scrum Half wants no "bad ball" from his forwards so an Outside Half wants no "rubbish" from his partner…

The key factor involves the distance in front of the Outside Half that the ball must be passed. This is greatly a matter of trial and error in the early stages. Even at International level, however, you will find the pair can benefit from going right back to basics and rebuilding confidence.

IV – TACTICAL KICKING OR KICKING FOR ADVANTAGE

Kicking away good possession is a last resort, but there are occasions when shrewd tactical kicking will bring the advantage…

With an inexperienced side, especially early in the season, it may be wise to try to play most of the game in the opposing half. To be sure, any pack of forwards will tell you that they prefer to be "going forwards", and this is the job of the tactical kicker. Obviously, we will want to make the maximum use of a strong wind or driving rain and to keep risk-play away from our own try line – and, of course, we may wish to kick to avoid opposing tacklers. The more the kicker can communicate with his own players, the better.

There are 4 main kicks to master:

i) High kick into the Box

Usually from the Scrum Half, over his pack or line out, so that his players can drive forwards onto the ball. Often the Blind Side Winger will be able to chase and harry. (NB. He is crucial in putting the pack on side. If possible, he will be warned that the kick is coming.)

This is an important kick to practise for a wet day ploy…

ii) High up and under (The Garryowen.)

Much the same as above but directed more centrally, usually for Centres to pursue and to put pressure on an isolated Full Back. Centres will try to get under the ball, catch it and make it available to the support players…

iii) Diagonal Kick

Outside Half or Inside Centre kicks diagonally, behind the opposing Winger. If your own wing man is alert, he stands a fair chance of getting to the ball first.

iv) Chip or Grubber

I don't like the Chip (little kick over opposite backs…) because it so often seems to give the opponent an easy catch and a free run. The **Grubber** (or push through the gap…) is usually more rewarding but it, too, is easily gathered or hacked forward by an alert Full Back. The Grubber is often effective on a wet or windy day when lofted kicks become unpredictable…

v – THE KICK-OFF

Re-starting the game with a **Place-Kick** or a **Drop Out**.

Coaching details will be as in KICKING SKILLS (Chapter 4) but it is worth re-emphasising the importance of this skill. Top line players spend ages working on precisely the right height and "float" needed for the chasing ball winners to regain control. It is a crucial and much underpractised area of the game… We should always be thinking in terms of regaining control from every kick-off…

Two practices to work on.
Practice 1: place markers on the pitch and learn to land the ball exactly on the spot.

Practice 2: practise the kick-off with your specialist players… and don't omit the occasional, unexpected switch kick-off to an unmarked, speedy winger on the other side of the field…

Andy Gomarsall – high kick into the box.

A young player showing excellent balance in the Drop Out.

THE XV IN ATTACK

**Including: i) Threequarter basics, ii) Beating your man
iii) Forwards on the charge, iv) Forwards in close support**

A 15-MAN RUNNING GAME

 This chapter focuses on encouraging a 15-man running game and it welcomes recent change in emphasis towards this more open style of play by the very best World teams…

In years gone by, this chapter would have been called "Threequarters in Attack" but that would be to miss the important change in the game. Nowadays, we expect all our forwards to run like gazelles (or rhinos) and to be every bit as involved in attacking moves as our strike players. Forwards can be crucial in committing more than one opposition back to the tackle, so opening gaps or creating overlaps. It is all about team strategy, dynamism and speed of thought…

TONY UNDERWOOD
Newcastle Gosforth, England and 1997 British Lions

SUPPORT PLAY

 In recent years, the art of support play, especially by the forwards has moved into interesting new territory. Today's fitness standards mean that the game is getting faster. My job, as the Openside Wing-forward, demands that I am frequently the first support man; the person who must be close to the ball-carrier and in a position to keep the movement going. Support play is about linking backs and forwards in attack…

NEIL BACK.
Leicester, England and 1997 British Lions

ATTACKING MOVES

 Attacking rugby is what we all want to play – but it needs to be based on sound foundations. To attack without precision seldom makes headway. Our strike runners stand a far better chance of success if the opposition defence is disorganised, thus we need the team to keep working through second, third or even fourth phase ball in order to put a man into space...

Careful study of this chapter will help but, essentially, look for self confidence and the right moment to strike – key factors in launching attacking moves. **99**

JOHN SLEIGHTHOLME
Bath and England.

TOTAL RUGBY – THE OPEN GAME

We hear a great deal about "15-man rugby", about the "expansive game", about "running rugby". Essentially, what every enthusiast wants is an exciting contest, if possible involving all 30 players – but there are a number of misconceptions...

To outlaw the kicking game completely is to misunderstand the skills and purpose behind the tactic. Just as there is a time and a place for a back row move, a forward drive or a rolling maul, so there is the moment for a tactical kick. To run the ball "blindly" is a passport towards failure and is not the key to a more expansive game. Nine times out of ten, the exciting, 15-man game comes from a XV winning quick, controlled ball – often ruck ball – which allows the back division time and space... The key to Total Rugby is that all the players are multi-skilled; they have the ability to retain possession and to maintain an attack when less skilful sides must opt for safety.

This chapter is about The XV in Attack but we must look first at a few basics...

i – THREEQUARTER BASICS

Make sure that every member of the Back Line agrees the following basics.

Get into attack formation immediately;
- Everybody takes their lead from the Outside Half.
- Be balanced as you take the ball – controlled, ready to sprint.
- Take early and use your fingertips.
- **Run and Pass with purpose**.
- Give your next man a bit more space or time to allow him to make his next decision.
- Pass at once unless you (or the next man) aim to break.
- *You remain responsible for the ball until the player you have passed to has used it effectively.*
- Pass and back up at once.
- *If tackled, it is your job to ensure that the ball remains available to your own side.*

ii – BEATING YOUR MAN

The individual challenge of man against man is perhaps the most compelling reason we have for playing this game. Sometimes we use **Team Strategy** or **Moves** to out-manoeuvre opponents; sometimes we rely on our own natural pace, power or flair. Normally, we expect to compete against an **Organised Defence** (at First Phase) – and probably also at the Second Phase. However, if we can win Third or Fourth Phase ball we should be expecting to score…

If you have a man with electric pace or the power to break tackles you will want to use him. Team strategy is all about manoeuvring the opposition to give your strike players this split second opportunity…

a) Switch or Scissors + the Dummy-Scissors
- Practise in pairs. One on the touch line; one on the 5m line. Walk it through.
- Receiving player must delay coming in as long as possible (ie. Don't tell your opponent what you intend…)
- Reach for the ball as it is offered. (The movement of the hand is often enough to convince an opponent that the ball is moving…)
- Ball carrier always turns towards the receiver; looks at him; offers him the ball. (Offer it; do not toss it.);
- Get close enough to deceive your opposition…

The **Dummy-Scissors** can be especially effective if it attempted soon after a real **Scissors** move.

b) The Loop
Be closer than usual to give yourself a chance to move into position for the second pass. You can loop with the next man in your line or you can loop round further out…

Forwards on the charge. Lawrence Dallaglio running in to score against France.

c) Draw a man and give a Pop-up Pass

This is all about timing – **and running straight**. Get on a line parallel with the touchline…

You draw your man by forcing him to come to take you; you do not want him to tackle you until your own support runner is in position and you may have to slow your forward momentum a bit. As your man comes through close and at speed, you will pop the pass for him to take. It may come as you are tackled; it may come as you are falling…

d) Introduce the extra man

The possibilities are enormous but it needs planning. Blind-side wingers or swift forwards or the Full Back are all available to make the extra man but the skill is to surprise your opponents. The key is timing. When should the "extra" man begin his run…?

Force him to tackle you.

Draw your man and look for close support runners.

iii – FORWARDS ON THE CHARGE

Balanced XV's expect to attack from backs or forwards. By and large we tend to use the forwards on the charge, to set up the second or third phase ball and disorganise the defence so that strike running backs can score. It is of course an unrealistic picture and every good forward will be looking for the scoring opportunity.

There are few more awe-inspiring sights (especially for an isolated Full Back trying to defend his line) than a pack of forwards on the rampage; skilfully interpassing and driving ever onwards at speed. It is enough here merely to emphasise the need for all forwards to practise the contact and close-passing skills; the quick rucking; the maul and the driving maul and to think very positively about your role in attack. Your first task is to win possession and for that reason your coach is sure to give early priority to set scrummage work and lineout work. That is essential. But after that – comes the main assault…

When the forwards are on the charge

- In attack – don't fan out across the pitch. Preserve a narrow front. ("Get behind the number plate of the player in front of you…") You can call "left" or "right" as you accelerate to take the ball…
- Depth is essential to inject pace.
- Try to adopt an aggressive body position: shoulders low, high knee lift… Terrify the opposition!

And get the ball round early as you approach the tackler. It must not be lost…

iv – THE BACK ROW IN CLOSE SUPPORT

One tends to think of Back Row players as the hard men who produce the "big hit tackles". Whilst this is partly true, a closer study will show these key players as vital links in attacking play.

Every good forward will be looking for the scoring opportunity.

The **Openside Flanker**, in particular, is expected to be "on the ball" at all times. If an Outside Half is looking to pass, he should know that his Openside is with him, usually close to his inside shoulder. The No 8 will not be far away and the Blindside Flanker, having checked his blindside duties first, will be close behind. It is true to say that the best Back Rows hunt in threes – and it is remarkable how often all three are involved in the final moves when a score is made…

Our aim must be to get men to the ball carrier or to the break-down point ahead of the opposition. Superior fitness and determination give a great advantage but there is no substitute for being able to "read the game"; to judge where the ball is going and to get there ahead of the rest. Many of the game's outstanding Back Row players have this uncanny knack and have built their reputations on this…

Support play can be rehearsed to an extent. The support runner can be told where the ball is expected to go so that he can get across and make the extra man. Back Row players can break quickly from a scrummage – or a Blindside Winger can use his pace to join the line as a support runner. It takes organisation and communication – but above all, it takes great skill to perfect the timing and the most effective line of running… Easily the best way to improve these skills is to watch an expert in action. Don't watch the ball; watch the particular player and see how he takes the best running lines towards the action.

Neil Back – specialist openside flanker.

England v. France, Twickenham 1997. Jon Sleightholme finds Richard Hill in close support.

Full Back Tim Stimpson in attack. Note the close support of England's powerful forwards: Simon Shaw, Jason Leonard, Tim Rodber and (right) Martin Johnson.

THE XV IN DEFENCE

DEFENCE INTO ATTACK

 Controlled and aggressive defence can be decisive in a close game. You will have studied **Confident Tackling** *in Chapter 4. In this section, we are concerned with the overall team plan of defence…*

Whenever possible, think of defence as an attacking ploy. Try to put your opponent down before he reaches the 'gain line' (diag. p. 32). A well organised defence should be aiming to be first to the released ball and immediately turning defence into attack. I like to refer to 'attacking defences'…

LAWRENCE DALLAGLIO.
**Wasps Captain, England
and 1997 British Lions**

England v. New Zealand Barbarians. Lawrence Dallaglio stops his man.

TEAM DEFENCE

All XV players must learn to be strong tacklers and to understand their role in the team's defence patterns. A totally committed defence can upset even the most talented of running XV's but it takes only one missed tackle to throw a match…

Often, the first tackle is crucial.

JONATHAN CALLARD.
Bath and England

THE XV IN DEFENCE

The complete XV must be properly organised, to defend as well as to attack.

Every man in the team has a defensive duty. He must understand the key elements of *pressure, depth, cover and communication.* Controlled and aggressive defence can be decisive in a close game.

The following diagram needs to be understood by all players. You need to know about the **Advantage** or **Gain Line…**

a) Defence for the Back Row and the Scrum Half

If opponents try a break from the scrum or the back row:

On one side:
Scrum Half takes the first man; Flanker, the next.
On the other side:

Flanker takes the first man; No 8, the next.
Aim low in the tackle and drive back over the gain line. *Stop the move before the gain line.*

Tim Rodber – Smother Tackle – v. Scotland.

If the opposition goes wide:
Openside Flanker takes the Outside Half (and continues to follow the ball across the field… running slightly *outside* each ball-carrier in turn). No 8 will be the next there, watching for the step back *inside.* The **Scrum Half** covers deeper trying to get between the ball-carrier and his own line…

b) Outside Half and Centres.

Make sure you all agree the following:
i) Get into position immediately. Front foot just behind the off side line. (Back foot of the scrum; 10m at Lineout…) (Outside Half is responsible for setting this line…)
ii) Give your opponent as little space as possible.
iii) Keep inside your opponent. Force him to run outside you and thus into your strongest tackle line.
iv) Never go up ahead of the man inside you. The Outside Half should go up fast on his man – even if he then changes to a **Drift Defence** (and takes the Inside Centre…)
v) Start fast but arrive in balance for the controlled tackle.
vi) Agree to take the man who comes to you. If this policy is agreed, scissors or dummy scissors need not cause confusion…

vii) If your man passes, you support the player outside you. If your partner makes the tackle, your job is to get your hands on the ball. (Centres will often have to do this…)

viii) If a break is made **inside** you, turn with your man and stay with him.

ix) Put your man down. A half tackle which permits your opponent to get the ball away, must count as a failure. If you can, turn him so that the ball is where we want it, on our side.

x) After the tackle, get away from man and ball. Get up before you play it. Don't be penalised…

c) The Full Back and the Wingers. (The Back Three…)

The back three must work together to provide depth in defence. They also have the job of setting up many of the counter-attacks. When the ball is in the air, one player should call for it. If in any doubt, the player who is deeper should take it and the other two should get round behind him to give support or start the counter attack.

The **Full Back** is the central defender. As a rough guide, he should be in line with the opposition ball carrier and in a position where he can if necessary force that player to the outside… It is far easier to move forwards into the catch or the tackle and under no circumstances should you get too close. If you have to deal with a ball in the air, do everything you can to take it before it bounces… Never flyhack!

The **Openside Wing** has to balance his two jobs. He must be ready to get up fast and pressurise his opposition winger but he must also be alert to the long diagonal kick from their Outside Half or Inside Centre… As the Openside Wing moves up on his man, the Full Back will move across to cover and the Blindside Wing will drop deeper to cover the Full Back. The three work together and build confidence by frequent communication…

The **Blindside Wing** has a particularly difficult defensive role on the "narrow side" near his own line. He must be quite clear – along with his Scrum Half and Back Row – whether he should come in and take the man in possession, or stay out and take his own man. This must be agreed before the game… Normally, he should stay with his own man unless an opponent has a certain score…

d) Forward Cover Lines

Team defence requires every player to take part. Remember we are attacking their ball-carrier, retrieving the ball and then being in position to counter-attack. It takes great discipline and determination to get into position and it is essential not to waste energy by running the wrong lines…

Guidelines would include:

i) Get between the ball and your own line – quickly. Don't just follow the ball…

ii) If you are covering across the field, assume that the outside opponent will receive the ball. The first tackler must keep going out, knowing that anyone coming inside him will be taken by his next player…

iii) Keep your head up and watch play develop (ie. If a ruck has been won, head for the next likely breakdown. Anticipate play and get there…)

Will Greenwood, Leicester and the British Lions. A player to watch…

Don't try to play the game going backwards under pressure

Kill the loose ball

Set up a maul

Get organised

and then PLAY RUGBY.

SCRUMMAGING

THE IMPORTANCE OF THE FRONT FIVE

 It is not by chance that most successful teams can look towards the foundation of a powerful Front Five. Even with the Law changes – especially in the U.19 game (p 50. Quiz 4) – scrummaging remains vitally important. There is a psychological advantage gained by being part of the stronger pack and this undoubtedly influences the rest of the team.

Today's Front Five must be quick around the field – ready to get involved in defence and support play – like every other player in the team.

Front Five play, however, is not for everyone! It's an area of severe strain and constant knocks and if you aren't ready to compete, I'd leave it alone. You've got to enjoy a bit of a battle really!

GRAHAM ROWNTREE
Leicester, England and 1997 British Lions.

England v. Scotland 1997.

SCRUMMAGE DIAGRAMS AND CHECK POINTS   A

I – PUSHING POSITION

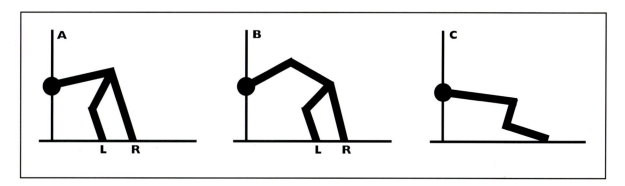

You want position C.

Hips below shoulders.

Chin forward to straighten back.

90 degrees between trunk and thighs.

90 degrees between thighs and lower leg.

Knees low.

Bind tight. Pull hard on waist bands and jerseys. Get tighter and lower than your opponents.

England team training. Note the flat spines – feet well back – heads up.

2 – STABILITY AND POWER

Feet wide, a little more than shoulder width (except for the Loose-head Prop who will be wider…) *This gives stability and allows use and transfer of power…*
Use your front 4 or 6 studs…

- Try to arch your back – hollow if possible. *This will straighten your spine to allow transfer of power/shove from behind.*
- Get as braced and tight as possible.
- **Look up! Look through your own scrum.** If you are staring at the grass – you're in the wrong position…
- **Force your head up.**

3 – TRANSFER OF POWER

The spines must be in line.

- **Start low**.
- Hips below shoulders.
- Get trunk lower by getting your knees nearer the ground. (Keep feet in the 90 degree position.)
- **On the 8-man drive** – get even lower.
- **If a Prop is in trouble** – get the hips lower and expect more support from your Wing Forward…

Jack Rowell supervising England.

5 – THE LOCK OUT

- On your own ball concentrate on the **Lock Out**; don't go backwards.
- Hooker strikes and everyone else…
- Drives into the locked position – and stays there.
- From here, your pack leader can call for a secondary drive…

4 – THE DRIVE

- At the moment of drive, drop the knees a little lower.
- Pick your head up and concentrate on driving **forwards and up**…
- Spine not merely flat, but depressed in the middle. Backside pushed out and back.
- "Squeeze! Knees! Now!"
- Try to direct the drive **inwards** towards the centre of the scrum, without impeding your hooker…

6 – THE FRONT ROW

6. THE FRONT ROW.

Shoulder height of the Front Row is vital. Get underneath…
(The Law requires that you do not "take the scrum down" but you want to try to get below your opponents and drive up into them…)
(Arm and neck strength – as well as lower body strength – is vital here.)

Tight Head leads into the scrummage.
Loose Head keeps the scrum high enough for the Hooker to see.
Tight Head stays low to restrict the view of their Hooker.

7 – ON THEIR BALL

- Get even lower.
- Eight men get feet back and drive.
- Flankers pack down straighter to assist forward momentum.
- Once in a while, the **Hooker** should have a go "*against the head*" but, essentially, you are aiming to give your opposing Scrum Half the worst ball possible.

If we can pinch the ball against the head, we will usually go for a No 8 pick up …

8 – BINDING

"Let's see the whites of your knuckles!" Get tight and then tighter…
Use the commands "Squeeze! Knees! Now!"
Re-tighten binding after initial contact with the opposition. Tight Head call "tighten" as soon as packs are down…
As the ball comes in, pull forwards on your colleagues' waist bands. Use your arm power!

YOU MAY NOT…

1. Kick the ball out of the tunnel
2. Handle the ball in the scrum
(unless for a Push Over try…)
3. Deliberately collapse the scrum
4. Deliberately fall or kneel in the scrum
5. Deliberately lift an opponent off his feet
6. Leave the scrum until the ball is out

Front Row. Good, wide position of the Loose Head.

B THE JOB OF THE HOOKER

The Hooker.

QUOTES FROM THE HOOKER...

" Hookers must be very competitive. A single ball lost, on our own put in, is a serious error…

Fitness is the key. The fitter man will always come out on top…

I seldom strike for the ball on their put in, usually we are concentrating on an 8-man drive and I think of myself as a third Prop…

Speed around the field is becoming more important. I have to train as an extra Flanker and expect to be heavily involved in support play and in defence…"

GRAHAM DAWE – Bath and England.

Bath pack in action.

Channel 1
For quick ball – but it puts your Scrum Half under pressure.

Channel 2
Controlled by No.8 + Scrum Half.
The normal route…

Hooker practice
Relax the striking leg; take all the weight off it.
Strike with the speed of a cobra! Aim beyond the ball.
Guide the ball back to your Scrum Half or No.8.

"A Hooker is no better than his Props…"
Work/talk with your Props every session. If they can put pressure on the opposing Hooker and upon the opposing binding – your life is that much easier.

Work with your Scrum Half to agree exactly how you want the ball put into the scrum. You need a code between you – probably just a movement of the hand…

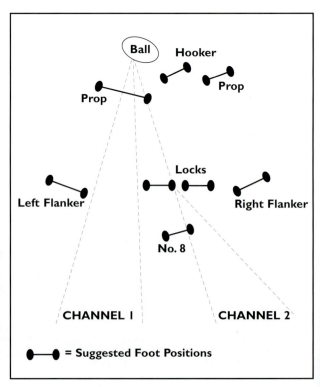

THE SCRUMMAGING BACK ROW   C

Page 29/30 examines the Back Row in Attack.
Page 32 looks at Defensive duties.
Here, we consider the work at the Scrummage…

Back Row scrummaging must be a sensitive balance between:
i) staying low and adding 100% support to the forward drive;
ii) staying low and helping to prevent any backward movement (the lock out);
iii) preparing to break – either in attack or defence.

Judgement is everything, and only years of experience will prevent you from taking wrong options. In the meantime – back your hunches! You learn by trying.

In simple terms, **Flankers** scrummage as hard as Locks! Their role is vital. We also expect the Back Row to be ever alert to control the sideways movement or the wheeling of the scrum. Only movement to our advantage should be permitted. Once the ball is away, the Flankers will be on the move… Add together all their duties and you have, most likely, the busiest men on the field.

Remember, all players must remain bound in – properly bound – until the ball is out of the scrum.

A **No.8's** scrummaging duties are less precise – indeed it takes great skill for a No.8 to make maximum contribution to the scrummage effectiveness. *Diagrams F and G on Page 36* give the basic requirement – but it is only experience which teaches a No.8 when to release the ball to his Scrum Half; when to urge his pack to drive forwards taking the ball at his feet or when to attempt a pick-up himself.

It is a fascinating and influential position.

A study of timing. Note that all legs are ready for the drive…

NINE

LINEOUT PLAY

Including: A) Our Ball, B) Their Ball

> *Quality lineout ball gives an excellent platform for attacking rugby. Poor or badly controlled ball is not worth winning… The thrower's accuracy is as vital as the ball winner; the jumper needs expert support players and immediate back up if he is to be successful; it demands concentration and team discipline…*
>
> *We need to face reality too. The higher up the competitive ladder you climb, the more difficult it becomes to referee the lineout precisely.*
>
> *A good side must quickly assess what a referee will or will not permit and adjust accordingly. As a ball winner, you are going to need great determination and skill; as with the scrummage, this is no place for the faint hearted.*

MARTIN JOHNSON.
Leicester, England and Captain of 1997 British Lions.

Tim Rodber winning the lineout for England.

OUR BALL   A

With the opposition Threequarter line obliged to be at least 10 metres back from the gain line, our own Backs must be given room to create and manoeuvre; our Forwards must have the option of using their Backs or of keeping the ball up front and driving onwards... In simple language, we MUST control the lineout.

Quality Lineout ball is most important; we want to 'guarantee' ball on our own throw... and get it to our Scrum Half with maximum advantage. (ie. quickly and under control). Frequently, we will make use of the sweeper or second touch man (see below).

It is, however, essential to realise that the lineout is little short of a battle ground! With two forward packs ready for combat and only a narrow gap of "no-man's-land" between them, it can be pictured as a kind of "trench warfare" with the spoils going to whichever side can win, capture or dominate the trench. Of course you must observe the referee's ruling, but equally you must discover precisely how close to this ruling you can tread without giving away a penalty. You can be quite sure that if your team does not control the "trench zone" – then the opposition will... **We need to be confident of winning three or four 'safe' throws:**

TRENCH ZONE

i) The fast throw or timed jump.
(The safest jump)

This is usually a quick throw to No.2 (our front jumper) who gets off the ground before the ball has left the fingertips of the thrower. The jumper must drive forwards and inwards. He must get into the space between the lines. For this throw, you aim to hit the jumper in mid-air. The thrower must practise; the arm should be cocked, ready to fire... Aim for the jumper's face. He will catch it!

ii) The jump in the middle of the line.
(Reserve safe catch)

This is another 'safe' jump; an attempt to put the ball in the middle of the Forwards – to be won by our own jumper, secured and then cleared up field. If stolen by the opposition, our players are well spread to defend against attack. This throw is usually a slower, flighted throw, and the classic "salmon's leap" to the very top of the receiver's jump. The "rock and roll jump" – the feint forwards, followed by the move back and up, must be checked with the thrower until perfect...

iii) Attacking peel from the long throw.
(The all-out attacking throw)

An exciting attack round the back of the line. Throw to be palmed down by the penultimate man (better than the very back man...) to a fast, powerful player coming round from the front. Sometimes it makes sense to play a strong flanker at Scrum Half for this move; he's ideally placed to run onto the palmed ball...

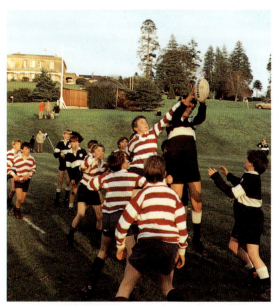

A two-handed catch at No. 2.

THE SWEEPER

This man becomes more important if his jumpers or Scrum Half are under severe pressure. (Normally No.1 sweeps back and 6 sweeps forward…) You have to be ready to take the palmed ball or the two-handed catch… You are the link between forwards and the Scrum Half and you will only come in to take the ball if this will help the Scrum Half… (i.e. an extra pair of hands on the ball may slow things down…)

Don't sweep until you have seen that the ball is where you want it. To move and then discover that the plan has gone wrong is a serious mistake…

THE THROWER

Pin-point accuracy is essential. Use whatever throwing method works best for you. Usually, the job goes to the Hooker – but I prefer to use the best thrower. It takes regular practice – first at a fixed target and then with your jumpers. Communication is vital.

The throw-in is crucial.

THE JUMPER

Concentration and determination!
- Take your cue from the thrower's arm – not from the ball.
- "*That's my ball*!" attitude is what it's all about. Drive up and at the ball.
- Power and spring can be improved with practice and training. See page 10.
- Success must be judged not on getting a hand onto the ball but on the quality of the ball you deliver to your Scrum Half or support player.
- Two hands are safer than one – but you can reach higher with one. Keep reminding yourself that "bad ball is forbidden…" – especially wet ball near your own line!

Good advice for jumpers will include:

i) Get in front of your man – even by an inch or two. Use your inside hip.

ii) Develop strong upper body (for wrestling the ball back) as well as a powerful leap.

iii) Never give up competing. Don't just jump and flap your arms…

iv) After a safe catch, begin to turn your body immediately, for delivery to Scrum Half or Sweeper, below waist height, or for a drive through the opposition.

Two hands are safer than one.

BLOCKING/SUPPORTING

(At the time of going to print, **Lifting** is forbidden in Under 15 Rugby.)

The referee is expected to penalise contact with your own team or with the opposition – before the ball has been touched by a jumper (i.e. you can't knock the guy over before he's touched the ball!) In practice it's a very difficult zone to get perfect and you need to play to the referee's interpretation…

However, all lineout players must understand that no-one comes through our line. There must be no way through the line to get to our Scrum Half.

Our Ball! Leicester Tigers in action. Martin Johnson with support from Graham Rowntree

The players immediately next to the jumper **must** protect him. They take their timing from the jumper's feet, moving in close, arms binding as tight as is possible to form a total barrier. Here, more than anywhere, we move into the "trench war-fare" zone and this is no place for the faint-hearted… The aim is to leave your jumper free to win and distribute the ball. The blocker behind the jumper should mimic the jumper's body angle. Press right up behind him and keep facing out, to follow play…

Whilst the immediate blockers protect the jumper, the rest of the pack also have work to do. The Scrum Half **must** be protected; a wall of tightly bound bodies "block" the opposition route through the line.

i) Attack the ball.

ii) Compress the line and allow no-one through.

iii) **Those at the ends** have the special duty (shared by the thrower) of ensuring that no-one comes round the line – so face your opponents. Don't turn your back on them…

This is crucial for the tail-gunner at the back of the lineout; he must protect his Outside Half from the opposition rhinos…

SIGNALS

These are the responsibility of the Pack Leader, working with **Thrower** and **Scrum Half**. Every player needs to know and understand the signals or calls…

SCRUM HALF POSITIONING

Don't get too close to your lineout. (About 5 or 6 feet as a guideline.)

• It is easier to come forwards than to retreat…

• Begin opposite the second or third man in the line – concealing where the ball is going.

B THEIR BALL

Attack their throw!

- Our Jumper to get in front of their man.

(It sometimes helps to move one man ahead of their jumper…)

- Get through or into their line. Our No.6 will attack their tap ball.

- At the back of the line – two players are detailed to think of cover: one checks that the Scrum Half has passed; the other goes for the Outside Half (and then the Centre…) Our Thrower is responsible for getting round the front to put pressure on their Scrum Half.

It is sometimes worth stacking the lineout with all our tall men around their most likely catcher. (ie. all around their No.2 jumper, if we are right on their line…)

If it's foul weather, we emphasise that we do not want any bad ball. We do, however, want them to have bad ball so we all need to compete and hassle them into errors…

SHORT LINE

Establish your "leaving order" to cope with their short line. Prepare for this and avoid the confusion which your opposition is hoping for.

DEFENCE AGAINST A PEEL MOVE

Stop this effective move before it gets going. The man best placed to put in the first tackle is your back lineout player, who goes forward to block their peeling man.

The England lineout.

RUCKING AND MAULING

Including: A) The Ruck, B) The Maul

" *Get there first! It's our ball and we need to ensure that we keep possession. Secure the ball and look for the back-up players. Whether it's a ruck or a maul, stay on your feet and keep the momentum driving forwards.*

In today's game, all players must be foragers and support players; everyone must be able to ruck or maul as needed – and we include these practices in every Club session. "

BEN CLARKE.
Bedford, England and the British Lions.

" *Strong rucking and mauling is an essential ingredient for every top side.*

We can all learn by studying the best – and, especially for the **Ruck,** *I point you again and again towards the* **All Blacks** *and their disciplined and awesome standards. Any young player can improve this part of his game by working on fitness and upper body strength – but at the end of the match it is all about determination, teamwork and self belief. The side which dominates here, will usually win.* "

TIM RODBER.
Northampton Captain, England and the 1997 Lions.

45

A THE RUCK

Even a light-weight pack can dominate by perfecting the rucking game. Indeed, at schoolboy level, the fast rucking game is very difficult to stop. We look for fast, driving packs who ground the ball when checked and ruck over, giving quick, clean ball for the backs. This puts the opposition back line on the retreat and, hopefully, in disarray; it's very exciting to play and to watch. For a side with superior fitness and gifted support runners it's a fine way to play the game.

Make sure you really understand this 1–6 practice routine:

i) Ball-carrier drives into coach/partner.
When he cannot maintain forward momentum, he half turns and forces the ball low and back.
ii) Support players drive in on either side, binding over the back of No.1.
These three players form the Front Row of the ruck.
iii) The next players (4 and 5) drive in binding on 2 and 3 and keep the momentum going.
iv) The ball is placed on the ground (not thrown) – maybe rolled slightly back – and the complete Ruck drives over and upwards, staying on its feet.
v) Any opponents who get into the way are used to bind on.
Make certain that no-one can slip through your Ruck.
vi) This will leave a clean, quick ball for your Scrum Half (or next player).

"Ball on the deck and drive over."

The **Ruck.**
Players have bound tight and driven over the ball.

Remember that forwards can pick up and drive themselves. Or they can pick up and pop a pass to a colleague. Judge the situation. How much space do you have? How close is the defence? Don't become predictable. Don't always just release to the Scrum Half and Threequarters...

The **All Blacks Rucking** advice...

Any rugby enthusiast will know of the All Blacks and their commitment to a fast, rugged rucking game. Check that you understand the following New Zealand instructions... Is there any difference to the 1-6 practice we've just looked at?

1. Drive beyond the ball.
2. Keep on your feet – keep your opponents on their feet.
3. Keep your eyes open.
4. Bind.
5. Come in low – and up.
6. Keep your balance.
7. Keep your spine "in line".

Aim for a 2-3-2 formation with the last man standing off (ready for the ball);
• hook in any other players anywhere near;
• as players arrive they must bend, bind, drive, with legs pumping hard with short strides; drive in hard – **Rucks go forward**;
• keep a strong firm unit – drive over the ball, leaving it alone for the Scrum Half...

THE MAUL   B

The purpose of the Maul is to retain the ball in the hands; you then have the option of safety play or an attack. Both need to be understood.

i – THE DEFENSIVE MAUL

To be set up under pressure.
No 1 – gets hold of the ball.
No 2 – moves in close to support (coming in from behind) and also gets hands on the ball.
No 3 – ensures that 2 has the ball and then concentrates on sealing off/protecting by binding in close and tight.
No 4 – does much the same but on the other side of the ball.
No 5 – can either add weight to the Maul or become the Scrum Half and call for the ball…

ii – THE ATTACKING OR ROLLING MAUL

Gain full control before beginning the roll.
Get the ball to the back, fast; it is then away from the opposition – and your Half Backs have sight of it…
i.e. As for Defensive Maul except that 5 stays close and bound in. Watch an expert team in action and you will realise just how difficult it is to stop. The man at the back can decide whether to release/retain the ball and drive/roll round the edges; break and charge…

"Get the ball to the back of the bus…"

Ball in hand – complete control.

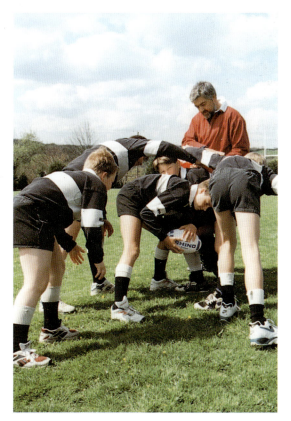

47

TEST YOUR RUGBY KNOWLEDGE

The four Quiz Sections which follow cover a wide range of Rugby Union knowledge.

They are **not** meant to be easy! Any young player who is able to find the correct answer to a good number of these questions will be heading in the right direction.

Please use the Quiz Section for **discussion** – and try to learn from it…

QUIZ 1 – Team Selection

QUIZ 2 – Mostly about Forward Play

QUIZ 3 – Mostly about Threequarters

QUIZ 4 – General Rugby knowledge & the laws

QUIZ 5 – Name the players

(Answers and/or page references are included – together with additional notes where helpful…)

Please note – these items are for **discussion** by all players. Sometimes there may be several reasonable answers and in many cases you will need to turn to the indicated page for fuller information.

12 or 13 year-olds are not expected to know all of the answers but they will do well to read, learn and discuss as much as possible. Any young player who is knowledgeable about all **test** sections will be better prepared than many senior club players…

Tick the boxes only if you understand and can explain or could demonstrate.

QUIZ 1

TEAM SELECTION

Write down the names of your strongest XV.
You may select from any team but you must be able to discuss the qualities required for selection in each position.

15. Full Back:

14. Right Wing:

13. Outside Centre:

12. Inside Centre:

11. Left Wing:

10. Fly Half:

9. Scrum Half:

1. Loose Head Prop:

2. Hooker:

3. Tight Head Prop:

4. Lock:

5. Lock:

6. Blind Side Flanker:

7. Open Side Flanker:

8. Number 8:

Replacements:

1	2
3	4
5	6

Your choice of Captain?

Now compare your team – and the requirements you have for each position – with a knowledgeable friend. If you have the knowledge to deal with this Quiz, you obviously know enough about the game to try Quiz 2…

QUIZ 2

Mostly about FORWARD PLAY

1. Explain what you understand by **Quality Possession** from scrum, lineout ☐

2. Consider the difference between the **Loose Head** and the **Tight Head Prop** ☐

3. Explain **Ruck** ☐
and **Maul** ☐

4. The different role of **Openside** and **Blindside Flankers** ☐

5. The **Off Side Law** at
i) Set Scrum ☐
ii) Ruck ☐
iii) Maul ☐
iv) Lineout ☐

6. Can you explain the meaning and importance of the following **Tight Scrummage** terms?
i) "against the head" ☐
ii) "secondary shove" ☐
iii) "binding" ☐
iv) "lock out" ☐

7. Why is **Second/Third Phase ball** so important? ☐

8. Can you explain…
i) Players going "over the top" ☐
ii) "turn-over ball" ☐

9. Explain the **Advantage/Gain Line** at
i) Set Scrum ☐
ii) Line out ☐

10. If the ball is thrown long, over the back of a **Lineout**, when can a player move to catch it? ☐

(Answers on page 52)

QUIZ 3

Mostly about THREEQUARTERS

1. Give three essential principles of **Back Defence** ☐

2. Explain the difference between **Man for Man** and **Drift Defence** ☐

3. When is it helpful to **Draw your man**? ☐

4. Explain the difference between and when to use the following **Kicks**:
i) Place ☐
ii) Drop ☐
iii) Screw ☐
iv) Grubber ☐
v) Garry Owen ☐

5. Can you demonstrate/explain the following ways of **Beating your man**:
i) Side Step ☐
ii) Change of Pace ☐
iii) Swerve ☐
iv) The Switch or Scissors ☐
v) The Dummy ☐
vi) Introducing the Extra Man ☐

6. Can you explain how the **Back Three** should work together in defence? ☐

7. What happens if a player deliberately throws the ball into touch or off the field of play? ☐

8. What do you understand by a **Smother Tackle**? When might you use it? ☐

9. How, when and where should you **Mark** a ball? ☐

10. Explain the advantages/disadvantages of passing flat or steep ☐

(Answers on page 52)

49

QUIZ 4

GENERAL RUGBY KNOWLEDGE & THE LAWS.

1. Name the current holders of the Rugby World Cup ❑

When and in what country will the next World Cup be held? ❑

2. In what way does the Under 19 Scrummage Law differ from that of Senior Rugby? ❑

3. Is it a try if:
i) A player touches down **on** (not over) the try line? ❑
ii) A player is held off the ground **over** the try line – and fails to ground the ball? ❑
iii) A player, diving for the try line, touches down before he is tackled into touch, knocking the corner flag over in the process? ❑

4. How many points are scored for
i) a try ❑
ii) a converted try ❑
iii) a drop-goal ❑
iv) a penalty? ❑

5. What should a **Referee** do if:
i) A player's studs are unsafe? ❑
ii) A player has committed a foul, but the opposition seems to have a good chance of scoring a try…? ❑
iii) He thinks that play is dangerous? ❑

6. Give the **definition** of a **Tackle** ❑
What must a tackled player do? ❑

7. After a try has been scored and the conversion has been missed, how should the game be re-started? ❑

8. Do you know why an unconscious person – or a player with a suspected neck or back injury should be moved **only** by a qualified expert…? ❑

9. What is the best way to treat a player who has been **winded**? ❑

10. Where must the ball come out of the **Scrummage**? ❑

(Answers on page 52)

QUIZ 5

NAME THE PLAYERS

Answers will be found on the page indicated.

Page 26

Page 27

Page 40

Page 30

Page 12

Page 30

Page 6

Page 25

Page 2

Page 40

TEST YOUR RUGBY KNOWLEDGE ANSWERS...

QUIZ 2 Answers

1) Quality possession: Ball delivered to the Scrum Half under control and as required.
2) Prop Forwards: Ch.8 page 36
3) Ch.10, Page 46. Ruck: ball on the ground. Maul: ball in the hand.
4) Back Row Defence: Ch.7 page 29/30 & 32.
5) Off side Law: Ch.4 page 19.
   i. set scrum: back foot;
   ii. ruck: back foot;
   iii. maul: behind the ball;
   iv. Line out: 10 metres.
6) i. "against the head": scrum ball won by the team not putting in the ball.
   ii. "secondary shove": The first shove "locks" the scrum and secures the ball; the team then regroups before calling for the "secondary drive" – usually with the No 8 controlling the ball with his feet.
   iii. "Binding": gripping another player's shirt or shorts to keep a tight unit.
   iv. "Lock Out": Ch.8 page 36
7) First Phase ball must be won against an organised defence. the defence should be in control.
   Second Phase will usually find your opponents less organised and by Third Phase the advantage may have passed to the attackers.
8) i. "over the top": If a team is likely to win ball on the ground, opponents can prevent the heel by diving over the ball. This is illegal and should be penalised with a penalty kick.
   ii. "Turn-over ball": a player who is tackled will try to ensure that the ball remains on the body side of his own team. A strong tackler can "turn over" the player as he tackles, thus making the ball available for his side.
9) Gain Line/ Tackle Line: diagram page 32.
10) Once the ball has left the fingers of the thrower.

QUIZ 3 Answers

1) Back Defence: Ch.7 pages 32/33
2) Man for Man is just that; you take your opposite number.
   Drift Defence means that if the opposition move the ball early, it may be possible for your Outside Half to come up on their Inside Centre and "drift" the defence across counter any extra opponents coming into the line.
3) When you want to ensure that he is not going to tackle the man you pass to...
4) See section on Kicking. Ch.4 Esp.16/17
5) Ch.6 pages 27/28.
6) See page 33. Full Back and wingers.
7) A penalty is awarded against him.
8) A tackle which prevents the man from passing the ball.
9) Ch.8 page 15 or see Index "fair catch."
10) Flat passing brings you closer to the gain line – but closer to the defenders. Study Ch.5 page 21.

QUIZ 4 Answers

1) South Africa. Wales 1999.
2) Under 19 Scrummage may not be driven more than 1.5 m.
3) i. Yes. On the line is a score.
   ii. No. He must ground the ball.
   iii. Yes. He scored before he went into touch.
4) i. 5, ii. 7, iii. 3, iv. 3.
5) i. Send him off to change them.
   ii. Play advantage. If they score – let it stand. If not – give a penalty at the place where the infringement took place. Either way, the referee should let the infringing player know that the offence has been noted.
   iii. Stop the game.
6) See Index. He must immediately release the ball and roll away from it.
7) A drop-out from the half-way line, by the non-scoring side.
8) You'll probably do serious damage if you move him.
9) Let him recover in his own time. Do not attempt to pump him up and down to "help".
10) Anywhere except at either end of the put-in tunnel.

INDEX OF NAMES AND RUGBY TERMS

* indicates International player in photograph or person contributing to the text

DROP OUT Means of restarting play from centre spot or 22m line.

DUMMY Pretend…

EXTRA MAN (Overlap) "Making an extra man" usually refers to the full-back or a powerful forward coming into the three-quarter line on attack, and thus making his wing an unopposed player *page 28*.

FAIR CATCH (or **MARK**) If a player makes a "fair catch" from a kick, a knock-on or a throw forward – within his 22m area – both feet on the ground – calling "Mark!" as he takes the catch, a free kick may be awarded. *Page 15*.

FITNESS *chapter 3*.

GAIN (ADVANTAGE) LINE An imaginary line drawn across the field through the centre of scrum, line-out, ruck or maul. An attack starts to be effective only when the ball is taken over the gain line. *Page 32*.

GARRYOWEN Up-and-Under kick named after the famous Irish club of the same name. High kick ahead designed to give your players time to follow up and cause confusion among defenders waiting for the ball to descend from the skies. The kicker must follow up ahead of his team mates to put them on side. *Page 23*.

*****GLANVILLE Phil de** *page 2*

*****GOMARSALL Andy** *page 22 and 24*

GOAL Combination of a try (5 points) and a successful conversion (2 points).

*****GRAYSON Paul** *page viii*

*****GREENWOOD Richard** *page iv.*

*****GREENWOOD Will** *page 33*

*****GUSCOTT Jeremy** *page 8*

HAND OFF A way of fending off a would be tackler by pushing him away with the open hand. It may not be a punch…

HALF TIME Time between halves. The Coach may come on to the field of play to advise players.

*****HEALEY Austin** *page 8*

*****HEALEY Dr. Norman** *page iii.*

*****JOHNSON Martin** *page ii, 40 and 43*

KNOCK-ON The ball bounces forwards off the hand or arm of a player attempting to catch or pick it up. Note the difference with "charge down".

LATE TACKLE Tackling a player after he has kicked or passed the ball. If done after a kick, the penalty will be awarded where the ball lands.

*****LEONARD Jason** *page 30 and 34*

LIFTING Gaining greater height for a lineout jumper by hoisting him.

LINE OF TOUCH An imaginary line in the field of play, at right angles to the touch line, through the place where the ball is to be thrown in at a lineout.

LOCK or **LOCKOUT** "Lock" is another name for "Second Row". Lockout *page 36*.

MARK See *FAIR CATCH*. The MARK is the place on the pitch where a free kick or penalty is awarded.

MAUL see *page 47*

MOUTH GUARD Recommended mouth protection – to be properly fitted by a qualified dentist.

OFF SIDE see *page 19*

*****OJOMOH Steve** *cover picture and page 3*

"OVER THE TOP" Preventing fair release of the ball. *Page 18, C(i)*.

PALM BACK A one handed deflection from the lineout (the inside hand must be used).

PEELING OFF A player from the lineout may "peel off" to take the "palm back" from a jumper…

PENALTY TRY Awarded when, in the opinion of the referee, a player would have scored if he had not been obstructed by a defender. The conversion kick is taken in front of the posts.

PROP FORWARDS Loose Head on the left. Tight Head on the right. *Page 37, 37 and 38.*

PUSH-OVER TRY When the attacking pack push the entire scrum back over their opponent's line and drop on the ball.

QUALITY POSSESSION Good, clean possession which we can use without being under pressure.

*RAW Michael *page vi*

*REAGAN Mark *page 34*

REPLACEMENTS Substitutes allowed to come onto the field to replace an injured player. Six are permitted at U.21 level.

*RICHARDS Dean *page 1*

*RODBER Tim *page 30, 40 and 45*

*ROWNTREE Graham *page 34*

*ROWELL Jack *page vii*

RUCK *page 46*

SCISSORS or **SWITCH MOVE** A pass where the receiver, instead of continuing in the same direction as the receiver, cuts back inside him. (Dummy scissors – the passer pretends to pass to the man on the "scissors".) *page 27.*

*SHAW Simon *page 30*

*SHEASBY Chris *page 19*

SMOTHER TACKLE A tackle in which the ball-carrier is not merely stopped but is caught with the ball so that he cannot pass it. *page 27.*

*STIMPSON Tim *page 30*

STUDS R.F.U. Safety regulations require studs of at least 10 mm diameter. Referees are expected to inspect studs before a game.

TACKLE To be "tackled", a player must be held (by one or more opponents) and **brought to ground** (or the ball into contact with the ground). NB. On one knee, both knees or sitting = tackled *page 13*

TAP KICK A tap-kick of only a few inches – made to himself – to restart play.

TORPEDO (SCREW KICK) A special spinning type of punt. *page 16*

TOUCH DOWN If a defending player grounds the ball in his own in-goal area, this is a touch down, and is followed by a drop out from the 22 line...

TOUCH IN GOAL When the ball goes out of play behind the goal-line.

TRAINING PROGRAMMES *Ch.3, pages 7–11.*

TURN OVER BALL turning the tackled player over the ball so as to leave the ball on your own side.

*UNDERWOOD Tony *page 25*

*UNDERWOOD Rory *page 12*

WHEELING THE SCRUM Turning the scrum so that it is sideways across the pitch. Usually a spoiling tactic to prevent opponents winning good ball.